Ten I
about J

ex libris

Candlestick Press

Published by:

Candlestick Press,
Diversity House, 72 Nottingham Road, Arnold, Nottingham NG5 6LF
www.candlestickpress.co.uk

Design and typesetting by Craig Twigg

Printed by Ratcliff & Roper Print Group, Nottinghamshire, UK

Selection and Introduction © John Foggin, 2022

Cover illustration © Gail Brodholt, 2022
www.gailbrodholt.com

Candlestick Press monogram © Barbara Shaw, 2008

© Candlestick Press, 2022

ISBN 978 1 913627 17 1

Acknowledgements

The poems in this pamphlet are reprinted from the following books, all by
permission of the publishers listed unless stated otherwise. Every effort has been
made to trace the copyright holders of the poems published in this book. The
editor and publisher apologise if any material has been included without
permission or without the appropriate acknowledgement, and would be glad to be
told of anyone who has not been consulted.

Thanks are due to all the copyright holders cited below for their kind permission:

Jean Atkin, *The Bicycles of Ice & Salt* (Indigo Dreams, 2021) by kind permission
of the author. Jo Bell, *Kith* (Nine Arches Press, 2019). David Constantine,
Madder (Bloodaxe Books, 1987) by kind permission of the author. John Foggin,
Pressed for Time (Calder Valley Press, 2022) by kind permission of the author.
Norman MacCaig, *The Many Days: Selected Poems of Norman MacCaig*
(Polygon Press, 2022). Michael McCarthy, *At the Races* (Smith/Doorstop, 2009).
Kim Moore, *If We Could Speak Like Wolves* (Smith/Doorstop, 2012). Sheenagh
Pugh, *Id's Hospit* (Seren Books, 1997). Rabrindranath Tagore, *I Won't Let You
Go: Selected Poems, New Expanded Edition*, trans Ketaki Kushari Dyson
(Bloodaxe Books, 2010) www.bloodaxebooks.com

All permissions cleared courtesy of Suzanne Fairless-Aitken
c/o Swift Permissions swiftpermissions@gmail.com

Where poets are no longer living, their dates are given.

Introduction

These days everyone on a TV trail of ancestry, or winning a cookery competition, has been on "quite a journey". It's a cliché, but at the heart of it is a truth we understand: that journeys should be in some way transformative...

A journey was once as far as you could travel in a day, and also a day's work. Journeymen were solid and reliable men paid by the day. A journal, like a log or a diary, is still an account of a day's doings. What poetry does, in its essential work of making us see afresh, is enrich the meaning of keywords. Ones like journey.

Words shift. A journey is more than just travelling. A journey is always a story made of episodes, stoppages, and epiphanies like those in Kim Moore's 'Train Journey, Barrow to Sheffield'. You can take a punt on losing your way on a journey, as in Jo Bell's 'Given', and equally, like Tagore in 'Journey Home', you can spend a life journeying to find your true self.

Jean Atkin's 'The bicycles of ice and salt' remembers this kind of vision in the Bildungsroman of a long-ago winter journey through France. Michael McCarthy reminds us in 'To School' that when you are young the most familiar landscapes are defined by the histories of its people. You journey through your growing story and if it makes you late for school there's no harm done.

What I've tried to do is hint at a world of poetry that shines light on the experience of the quest, on the involuntary journey, on journeys (like life) into the unknown and full of roads not taken, avoided by our inner Billy Liar in David Constantine's 'London Road' or, as with Chaucer's tale, a journey as a pilgrimage which is also a jaunt, the medieval equivalent of a cruise or a coach tour.

If you're lucky, it will have a happy ending. Maybe someone like Norman MacCaig in 'July landing' will be on the shore, watching for your arrival. Shakespeare's Feste was convinced of it: "Journeys end in lovers meeting / Every wise man's son doth know".

John Foggin

What If This Road

What if this road, that has held no surprises
these many years, decided not to go
home after all; what if it could turn
left or right with no more ado
than a kite-tail? What if its tarry skin
were like a long, supple bolt of cloth,
that is shaken and rolled out, and takes
a new shape from the contours beneath?
And if it chose to lay itself down
in a new way; around a blind corner,
across hills you must climb without knowing
what's on the other side; who would not hanker
to be going, at all risks? Who wants to know
a story's end, or where a road will go?

Sheenagh Pugh

To School

Summer time and the short sleeves, and no shoes
and rabbits bobbing west-side of Sean Neill's bog.
Dew on the grass, and the gap in the ditch,
and frog spawn in the long-go flax pond,
and the water-works and the briars by the big tank
and smoke from Johnny Noonan's one chimney.
The faucet like a small fountain beside the river
where Mrs Noonan gets the water for their tea,
where we drum our feet on the wooden bridge

and race up Kingston's field past the stall and the shed,
the house and cherry tree, and down to Carraig a Thonnaig.
'Your father slept there during the troubles,' Willie says.
Then up the hill past the hazel tree and the high ditch
to the rutted road, and away below us the river's rush.

Across the valley Harnedy's house hides in the trees.
We catch up to Den Brien on his way to the creamery
with his slow horse and iron wheel cart and churns
that clang as he goes along, and Den deaf as a stone.
He tells us to sit in. The big iron wheels turn slowly,
the churns lurch at every turn, we fear for our fingers
and toes. It takes forever to get up Paul Sam Jim's hill.
At Dempsey's gravel pit we know we'll be dead late,
like being after the Gospel getting into Mass.

At Miah Charley's cross Den pulls in, lets
Jim Carthy swish past in his rubber wheeled cart.
At Chrioshe na Marb there's no sound because
they've all gone in to school. He lets us off
at the humped back bridge. We say thanks for the lift.
The master will surely give us a slap.

Michael McCarthy (1945 – 2018)

Given

A dark man gave me this, and it was everything:
a cabin twelve by six, and Severn rising limitless.
No romance, no quarter; little rest.

In his coffin bunk, our skins, the channels of my wrist
were specks of engine oil and wine, small piracies of self.
We made a travellers' pact to go wherever water let us pass,
together until each stood in the other's way.

His second gift was a clean parting. Love passes,
water stays. Inconstant: always borrowed, never spent.
A better woman would be sorry now.

Jo Bell

Journey Home

The time that my journey takes is long and the way of it long.

I came out on the chariot of the first gleam of light, and pursued my voyage through the wildernesses of worlds leaving my track on many a star and planet.

It is the most distant course that comes nearest to thyself, and that training is the most intricate which leads to the utter simplicity of a tune.

The traveller has to knock at every alien door to come to his own, and one has to wander through all the outer worlds to reach the innermost shrine at the end.

My eyes strayed far and wide before I shut them and said 'Here art thou!'

The question and the cry 'Oh, where?' melt into tears of a thousand streams and deluge the world with the flood of the assurance 'I am!'

Rabindranath Tagore (1861 – 1941)

The bicycles of ice and salt

Green panniers strapped and hooked to racks
we pedal the east of France, this autumn so bitter
the bicycles grow ice in their chains.

They sing like birds, says a lyrical
bike mechanic in Troyes. He hoses them down
with hot water, and they go quiet.

We ride through white bees of hoarfrost
that blur our eyelashes. Ice narrows us.
We count the centimes

double the bread ration, camp
in a numb cold. In Avignon the mistral
rips up our tent pegs, hurls us south.

We ride till our freewheels tick on a track
to the sea. December, and a beach
washed black by short days.

Glassy waves crash in the dark. We hear them
break. There is no more ice, only a swell
of salt to melt the heart.

Jean Atkin

Train Journey, Barrow to Sheffield

Even though the train is usually full of people
I don't like, who play music obnoxiously loud
or talk into their phones and tell the whole carriage
and their mother how they're afraid of dying
even though they're only twenty five,

even though the fluorescent lights
and the dark outside make my face look like
a dinner plate, even though it's always cold
around my ankles and there's chewing gum
stuck to the table and the guard is rude

and bashes me with his ticket box,
even though the toilet smells like nothing
will ever be clean again, even though
the voice that announces the stations
says Bancaster instead of Lancaster,

still I love the train, its sheer unstoppability,
its relentless pressing on, the way the track
stretches its limb across the estuary
as the sheep eat greedily at the salty grass,
and thinking that if the sheep aren't rounded up

will they stand and let the tide come in, because
that's what sheep do, they don't save themselves,
and knowing people have drowned out there
like the father who put his son on his shoulders
as the water rose past his knees and waist and chest

and rang the coast guard, who talked to him
and tried to find him, but the fog came down,
and though he could hear the road, he didn't know
which way to turn, but in a train, there are no choices,
just one direction, one decision you must stick to.

This morning the sun came up in Bolton and all
the sky was red, and a man in a suit fell asleep
and dribbled on my shoulder till the trolley
came round and rattled loudly and he woke up
with a start and shouted *I've got to find the sword.*

Kim Moore

from The Prologue to The Canterbury Tales

When in April the sweet showers fall
And pierce the drought of March to the root, and all
The veins are bathed in liquor of such power
As brings about the engendering of the flower,
When also Zephyrus with his sweet breath
Exhales an air in every grove and heath
Upon the tender shoots, and the young sun
His half-course in the sign of the *Ram* has run,
And the small fowl are making melody
That sleep away the night with open eye
(So nature pricks them and their heart engages)
Then people long to go on pilgrimages
And palmers long to seek the stranger strands
Of far-off saints, hallowed in sundry lands,
And specially, from every shire's end
Of England, down to Canterbury they wend
To seek the holy blissful martyr, quick
To give his help to them when they were sick.

It happened in that season that one day
In Southwark, at *The Tabard*, as I lay
Ready to go on pilgrimage and start
For Canterbury, most devout at heart,
At night there came into that hostelry
Some nine and twenty in a company
Of sundry folk happening then to fall
In fellowship, and they were pilgrims all
That towards Canterbury meant to ride.

Geoffrey Chaucer (1340 – 1400)

London Road

Even the signpost's gone
That stood here pointing which way
London was and the miles,
One hundred and eighty-six,

With a finger. Then the road
Smiled and hitched up its pants
And put its best foot forward
And sloughed all this here off:

The blinded warehouses,
The shops doing badly,
The chapels doing worse, the big
Empty Majestic, all the slag.

For the road believed
The friendly hand and the pointing finger
Their definite number of miles
And shouldered its bundle on a stick.

Yes, said the standing post,
In the voice of a blackened elder,
There's nothing but fields now,
You'll get your strength up marching,

You'll get some air, you'll be fit
For the folks in London to look at.
Go on, son, you can do it,
Though none of us ever did.

David Constantine

Out there

How we are drawn to edges; to sweeps of pale sand;
to the banks of rivers to watch the waters endlessly process,
to marvel, without knowing why, at boats
and at those who know the ways of boats and of water;
to sea shores, brown estuaries, white cliffs, and most of all
to the farthest west, to dream of the drowned.

Imagine yourself a goldcrest, comfortable in a cushion of down
between an eagle's shoulder bones, high over Cader Idris,
you'd see, you think, the drowned lands of Cantre'r Gwaelod
pale silver in a shallow sea. Or high over brown Bodmin
the sun going down in a fume and the pinnacles of Lyonesse,
and the lost world of Ys, scattering gold in a molten flux.

Imagine yourself a white horse to follow the track of the sun
west over seas to sink in the dream of Tír na nÓg
where no one shall grow old. Understand you can not come back.
The weight of lost years falls on those whose feet touch the earth.

We take strange comfort in all this.
If we were white horses we would settle for the earth.
If we were birds, edges would mean nothing.
We would know no boundaries.

John Foggin

July landing

The *Eilean Glas*, engine full ahead,
slavers through the sea, wolfishly
making for its lair
at Lochinver. It brushes aside
the sparkling splinters of water.

The day is wildernesses, all
desolate and lovely...
As monumental as a monument
a blonde sheltie drowsily stares
through filmstar eyelashes
at the road hemstitched on the skirt
of a mountain. Somewhere
a lamb laments
with the voice of desolation.

On the sand at Clashnessie
six sandpipers play tig
with the Minch, that
keeps casting up and withdrawing
a rinse of soiled lace infested
with sandgrains.

And round Stoer Point swirls
a typhoon of gulls and, under it, the *Eilean Glas*
grinning through the water
till it comes to rest at the pier
in a green seethe of watery
mushrooms and Catherine wheels
and the engine stops
with a clap of silence.

Norman MacCaig (1910 – 1996)